# The Happy Sales System

Close More Deals with a Stress-Free Sales Process
Designed for Genuine Human Beings

Sean Dudayev

Copyright © 2024 by Sean Dudayev

All Rights Reserved. Except as permitted under the U.S. Copyright Act of 1976, no part of this publication may be reproduced, distributed, or transmitted in any form or by any means, or stored in a database or retrieval system, without the prior written permission of the publisher.

Any unauthorized copying, translation, duplication, importation, or distribution, in whole or in part, by any means, including electronic copying, storage, or transmission, is a violation or applicable laws.

# Table of Contents

Introduction .................................................................. v

   Before You Start Selling ........................................ viii

## The Happy Sales Process ........................................... 1

   Step 1: Make a Friend ............................................... 2

   Step 2: Alleviate the Fear of Uncertainty ................. 3

   Step 3: Discovery ....................................................... 5

   Step 4: Build Value .................................................... 8

   Step 5: Build Trust ................................................... 13

   Step 6: Light the Path Forward ............................... 15

   Step 7: Follow up .................................................... 20

## Happy Prospecting Process ..................................... 24

   Know What You're Selling ..................................... 24

   Have an Offer .......................................................... 25

   Craft the Pitch ......................................................... 25

   If They Say No - 2nd Attempt ................................ 27

   If They Say Yes - Discovery ................................... 28

   Book the Time ........................................................ 28

   Light the Path Forward .......................................... 29

   Sell the Sales Call .................................................... 29

## Happy Sales Principles .................................................. 34

### Acknowledge the Fourth Wall ........................................ 34
### Pre-Buttal, Not Rebuttal .................................................. 37
### Pressure to Speak is On You .......................................... 39
### Always Be Enthusiastic ................................................... 41
### Follow up ............................................................................ 43
### Don't Disappear After the Sale ..................................... 45
### Play the Numbers ............................................................ 46
### Track the Numbers ......................................................... 48
### Make the Most of the Numbers ................................... 49
### Maintain Mental and Physical Health ........................ 52
### Don't Take it Personally ................................................. 55

## The Ceiling is You .................................................................. 56

## A Message to Salespeople .................................................. 57

## A Message to Business Owners ........................................ 59
### What I Know About You ................................................ 60

## Happy Selling ......................................................................... 61

## About the Author .................................................................. 62

# Introduction

I know the feeling.

You sit there watching YouTube videos, reading sales books, and talking with sales managers. They all share these awkward, super-aggressive sales tips to help you close more deals. But it all feels wrong to you, going against your natural instincts.

You don't want to follow these strategies because they seem slimy and disingenuous.

"This can't be it," you think. "Maybe I'm just not cut out for sales?"

For decades, we've been taught that pushing people into decisions, making them doubt themselves, and using every psychological trick in the book is how to be a "closer."

This is how you "bring home the bacon." The worst part is these gurus use the same tactics on you to make you adopt their methods. If you resist, they accuse you of not caring about your family.

And then there's that one guy who makes people take off their shirts on stage, trying to link levels of fitness with sales success.

It's all nonsense. Most of the time, the techniques you are being taught aren't being used in practice.

I've worked with hundreds of salespeople, and I've seen a 60-year-old Southern woman, who didn't fit the aggressive sales mold, outsell an entire team of hard-hitting "closers." All she did was genuinely care for her prospects.

I'm not dismissing the importance of psychology in sales. Persuasion is an art with its own process.

That's because every human being has a little monkey in their brain that is afraid of change. Our job is to get around that monkey and explain to the human brain that this decision is a good one and that separating themselves from their resources (money) will give them a much bigger benefit in return.

There's a way to do this without compromising your values to make a sale.

The biggest challenge these ethically questionable sales gurus face today is that consumers are much more educated and have countless options. They know they don't have to buy from you and can see through any act. You're no longer the only salesperson around. Your prospects have access to salespeople from around the world.

Despite the criticism we often hear about Millennials and Gen Z, they are incredibly perceptive and have access to more information than any previous generation.

They're more likely to be manipulated by an influencer than by a salesperson. So, unless you have millions of followers, you need to adopt an ethical sales process that treats prospects as people, not transactions.

In this book, I am going to show you a process that I have carefully crafted over 18 years in sales.

I've successfully sold just about everything including:

- Insurance Products
- Alarm Systems
- Credit Counseling Services
- SaaS Products
- Marketing Services
- Sales Consulting Services
- Real Estate
- Speaking Engagements
- Partnerships

And, of course, selling myself.

I've sold in various settings: face-to-face, over the phone, and through Zoom. What I've learned is that the same sales psychology applies regardless of what you're selling or the medium you use.

This sales process doesn't rely on outdated, pushy tactics. You don't need to force products and services onto people.

The Happy Sales System is a stress-free, seamless approach that every salesperson will love. It helps you close more business without the usual antics.

Here's what you'll discover next:

- The Happy Sales Process
- Happy Prospecting Tips
- Happy Sales Principles
- A Little Sales Motivation
- Parting Words

There's no fluff in this book, just effective tips that won't leave you feeling uneasy after a sales call. A short, easy, and impactful read.

This book is for salespeople who want to be happy in their work. Happy because they're making money, and happy because they can be themselves while doing so.

## Before You Start Selling

Sales is about offering a solution to the consumer. You need to clearly and effectively show them, step by step, that not only do you have a solution to their problem, but you have the best solution.

To do this well, every salesperson must have one crucial element: deep product and service knowledge.

If you don't know enough about what you're selling, you're not being an ethical salesperson. You're not serving your prospects properly. Without investing time to understand your product or service thoroughly, you can't grasp the problems your prospects face or how your solution can help them.

Even if you don't excel at anything else in sales, mastering this will set you up for success.

To become proficient, immerse yourself in learning about your product. Read everything available, ask the product team questions, talk to the creator, and consult the marketing team. Review every piece of marketing material and customer feedback. Ensure everyone involved in creating and marketing the product can address any concerns or misunderstandings. You need to be well-versed in both the strengths and weaknesses of your offer.

Depending on what you're selling, this learning process might take a day, a week, or a month. However long it takes, make it your top priority.

I'm not saying to stop prospecting and making money, but if you've been selling a product for months without this depth of knowledge, start fresh as if you're a beginner.

Customer reviews are particularly insightful. They reveal what people love, like, or dislike about your product, which helps you better qualify your prospects.

Also, study your top competitors. Understand their features, benefits, and their good and bad reviews. Know every competing offer your customer might consider, and analyze where your product stands in comparison.

Your goal isn't just to get people to pay. It's to get them to stay.

Don't leave this solely to customer service. Despite what executives might think, creating loyal customers begins with sales, is supported by service, and is reinforced by the product. If the customer builds a strong rapport with the salesperson and is well-informed, they're more likely to overlook any issues later on.

It might seem obvious that you need to know your product well, but it's vital to do your due diligence. The basic training materials or brochures you received in your first week aren't enough.

Go the extra mile.

A sales call is like a fight. All your preparation is intentional, but during the call, your mind reacts in split seconds, operating on autopilot. Your responses are based on your training. If you don't want to get caught off guard, you must be well-prepared. Just as a fighter senses their opponent's hesitation, a prospect can tell when you're uncertain or insecure about your knowledge.

The cure is to be well-informed so there are no surprises. Your aim is to have a wealth of knowledge ready to draw from during the sales call.

Before diving into The Happy Sales System, make sure you fully understand your product. The rest of this book will be much more valuable if you do that first.

Now, let's jump into the sales process that will help you close more deals and feel more confident as a salesperson.

# The Happy Sales Process

A good sales process involves caring for your prospect just as you would for your best friend.

Imagine your friend has a problem. You'd likely start by asking them some questions to understand their situation better and see if you can help. After getting a clear picture of their issue, you might suggest a solution. Knowing that your idea could genuinely solve their problem and improve their life, you'd feel confident in offering it.

If your friend initially said "no" to your suggestion, would you just drop it? Not if you truly cared about helping them. You'd ask more questions and explain why your solution is a good fit for their specific issue.

This approach is about influencing others for their benefit, something you've done many times in your life. The challenge in a sales call is the pressure of "selling" and the prospect being aware that you're trying to sell. This dynamic often makes you seem like you're on the offense and them on the defense.

In contrast, when talking to a friend, your conversation naturally flows like, "Hey, based on what you're telling me, I think you should consider this solution because it will really help you avoid this problem."

This is why the first step of the sales process is ...

## Step 1: Make a Friend

At the beginning of every sales call, the first step is to establish a human connection.

Number one is always building rapport.

It doesn't matter if you're not an extrovert or lack charisma. No matter who you are, you can find a way to build rapport. It could be as simple as asking about the weather where they are or commenting on something relevant to their business, an event, the time of day, or just life in general.

A helpful "trick" is to be genuinely curious about the person you're speaking with. Pay attention to background noises or visual cues.

Do they have kids? A dog? Is there a guitar on their wall? These little details are parts of their life they're open to sharing. Ask them about it.

Everyone appreciates connection, even the most cynical people. That's why you build rapport first.

Remove the transactional nature of the call and create a human connection. You don't need scripted responses or special preparation for this. It's like the small talk you naturally make with people in an elevator or a coffee shop. Do this at the start of every sales interaction.

You're not just doing this for your prospects; you're doing it for yourself too. It helps you see the person on the other side, turning the call into a meaningful conversation rather than a cold transaction. It can become a mutually beneficial exchange between two people.

Create a warm environment for the call and add a personal touch.

The rapport-building process doesn't have to be long.

It could be a minute or ten minutes, depending on what feels natural.

Make a friend.

Don't buy into the cliché that business is separate from personal. Everything we do is personal. Keep your humanity, and you'll likely find more success. It's not only beneficial for everyone involved but also just good manners.

## Step 2: Alleviate the Fear of Uncertainty

Once you've established a connection, the next step is to ease any uncertainty your prospect might have. Even though we're civilized and self-aware, we still have a primal need to anticipate what's coming to avoid danger. When we meet someone new, our senses are on high alert, almost on autopilot.

Your role is to reduce this anxiety by clearly outlining what to expect next.

Right after building rapport, explain how the call will proceed. Don't leave anything out.

For example, when I'm selling my marketing or sales services, I say:

*So, here's what I'd like to do on this call:*

1. *Learn a bit more about you and what prompted this call.*
2. *Share some ideas on potential solutions.*
3. *Tell you a little more about us and answer any questions you have.*
4. *Determine if there's any value I can provide for you.*
5. *Finally, explain our process and how we work.*

*How does that sound?*

Always follow up a statement with a prompt for them to respond. Keep the conversation flowing and ensure the pressure to speak stays on you. Your prospect should feel like a hot knife gliding through butter – effortlessly at ease. Your goal is to make them comfortable with no moments of tension throughout the call.

I know this is different from traditional sales teachings, but you might need to let go of some of that "knowledge" if you want to be a happy salesperson.

This step is like taking their hand and reassuring them, "Come, it's safe this way."

## Go on a Date

Effective sales are a lot like effective dating. If you want your first date to potentially lead to a healthy long-term relationship, you shouldn't spend the entire time just trying to impress the other person. If you're smart and confident in your worth, you'll evaluate whether they're a good fit for you, too. The key to doing this is asking the right questions at the right times.

You also need to let them evaluate you to see if you're a good fit for them. This means answering their questions honestly, avoiding any false claims about your abilities, and clearly stating your boundaries about what you can't do.

Many salespeople make the mistake of putting their prospects on a pedestal, doing anything to win their favor.

This undermines your authority and puts you in the position of a beggar, causing them to lose confidence in you as a guide. They need to trust your judgment, but they can't do so if your only aim is to please them by saying what they want to hear.

You're not just trying to "wow" them. You're trying to determine if you can be of value to them, and if they are to be of any value to you.

Not every customer is the right customer.

This is what steps 3 and 4 help you accomplish.

## Step 3: Discovery

This is where you determine if the prospect is a good fit. While you can take some qualifying steps before the sales call, much of this evaluation happens during the call itself.

You can start the qualification process during prospecting, through lead forms, or by working with the outreach team. These early steps are essential for making your life easier.

However, these methods can't replace the needs analysis and discovery process that you, as the salesperson, must perform during each call. There are insights you can gather in a conversation that a cold call or lead form simply can't provide.

During discovery and needs analysis, you identify their hot buttons and pain points.

If you're new to sales, "hot buttons" are the solutions they're looking for or the specific features and benefits they want from your product. "Pain points" are the problems they're facing in their business or life that they need to solve.

Understanding these aspects allows you to tailor your presentation to their needs. That's why discovery must come before your presentation. You can't propose a solution without fully understanding the problem.

To transition from building rapport to discovery, start with a question:

When I sell my services, I usually ask:

*"Tell me more about your business, the challenges you're facing, and what prompted you to schedule this call?"*

If you already have some information, incorporate it into your question and ask them to expand or provide more details. This way, you avoid making them repeat themselves and show that you've been listening.

Let them talk freely and avoid interrupting their flow. If they miss answering any of the points, gently prompt them again. After they've spoken, summarize what they've told you. This confirms your understanding and ensures they feel heard.

In a good sales process, everything benefits both you and the prospect. A successful business transaction involves a near-equal exchange of value, leaving both parties satisfied.

Keep the conversation natural and ask as many questions as needed to gather enough knowledge to present a solution effectively.

Some effective questions include:

- What has worked for you in addressing these issues?
- What have you tried that hasn't worked?
- What was the tipping point that made you seek a solution?

These questions remind them that they have a problem and are actively seeking a solution. You're not there to force a sale but to help them find the right one.

Remember, the prospect is already on the call, meaning they need a solution. Your job isn't to convince them they need you; it's to remind them why they do.

The best way to influence someone's decision is to ensure it aligns with their best interests.

Each of these steps is crucial because they collectively help guide your prospect comfortably to the finish line, achieving the goal for both of you.

The next step is one of the most critical, where your product and industry knowledge must truly shine.

## Step 4: Build Value

No, this isn't the moment to talk about yourself, your accolades, or why you're so amazing—that comes later. This step is all about taking everything you've learned about your prospect and connecting it to your product or service as their solution. This is where you build value for them.

**For Products**

If you have a product, this is where you demo it. You have to make sure that as you go through your typical demo process, you're catering this demo specifically to their hot buttons and pain points. As you go through each feature, communicate what it does for them.

This is a multi-step formula, let's call it The Happy Formula:

1. The feature and what it does
2. What the feature does for them
3. How it solves their specific problem
4. There personal benefits that they can derive from it in their life/business

Here is a simple worksheet you can use to practice including this in your product demonstrations. This works for digital and physical products:

**Value Building Worksheet**
*Product/Feature:*
*Describe What It Is*

*Feature Description:(Provide a brief description of the product or feature)*

*Describe Its Function for Them*
*Function Description:(Explain what the product/feature does)*

*Describe How It Solves Their Problem*
*Problem-Solution Description:(Detail how the product/feature addresses a specific problem)*

*Discover the Practical Benefit*
*Practical Benefit:(Identify and describe the practical benefits, such as increased revenue, time-saving, cost reduction, etc.)*

*Describe the Emotional Benefit*
*Emotional Benefit:(Describe the emotional impact or benefit, such as feeling more secure, confident, happy, etc.)*

Take the time to fill this out and you will see a huge difference in how people respond to you during your demos.

Here is an example using headphones as a product:

*Describe What It Is*
*Feature Description: These are our latest noise-canceling headphones.*

*Describe Its Function for Them*
*Function Description: These headphones actively block external noise, allowing you to enjoy clear, uninterrupted sound.*

*Describe How It Solves Their Problem*

*Problem-Solution Description: If you frequently work in noisy environments or travel often, these headphones will eliminate distractions and help you focus.*

*Discover the Practical Benefit*
*Practical Benefit: By using these headphones, you can increase productivity and improve your listening experience, whether at work or leisure.*

*Describe the Emotional Benefit*
*Emotional Benefit: You will feel more relaxed and focused, enjoying a sense of peace in noisy environments. Your ability to get things done will also mean peace of mind when you're at rest.*

We're taught to communicate features and benefits, but the benefits of a product are multi-layered. You have to cater to different mindsets. Some people are more emotional, some people are logical, and some are a blend of creative and analytical. Your job as a happy salesperson is to make sure every single type of person can understand what your product does for them.

**For Services**

If you offer a service, this is your chance to showcase how well you understand their problem and how you would address it. Selling services requires quick thinking because your approach may vary depending on the different challenges your prospects face.

When I sell my services, I draw on my extensive experience in growing businesses and past successful projects. I relate directly to the client's challenges and discuss the specific strategies I would use to drive their growth.

This is no time to talk about your team or your company. Instead, focus on demonstrating your expertise as it pertains to their needs.

Think of it like the "Try Me" button on a children's toy—it gives a glimpse of what the toy can do before you buy it.

In service sales, your knowledge and expertise are your "Try Me" button. Showcase this knowledge boldly. Build your value and stand out from the competition.

While other salespeople might be talking about their company and why they're great, you should focus on their problem, the solution, and how you would tackle it. By now, you've spent the entire call focused on them. You've made a connection, learned about their needs, and now you're demonstrating how you can help. You're making them feel heard and valued, something many of us lack in our daily lives.

This is what 99% of salespeople don't do.

When selling services, use a similar approach to the product "features/benefits" pitch, but highlight what makes you unique for each benefit.

Explain how your service stands out from the competition.

To do this effectively, you need to understand what others in your industry often get wrong.

For instance, when I sell digital marketing services, I emphasize areas where many marketing agencies fall short:

- Most marketing agencies focus on vanity metrics; we prioritize the bottom line.
- Many agencies have poor communication; we provide bi-weekly reports, even when there's nothing new to report.
- Others ask for long-term commitments; we believe you should stay with us because we deliver great results, not because you're locked into a contract.

This is why the research phase is crucial. It helps you uncover what makes you different from others, which could be your biggest value proposition.

Here's an updated worksheet designed for companies selling services, including a section on how your service is distinct from other providers.

## Value Implementation Worksheet for Services

*Describe What It Is:*
*Service Description: (Provide a brief description of the service)*

*Describe Its Function for Them*
*Function Description: (Explain what the service does for the customer)*

*Describe How It Solves Their Problem*
*Problem-Solution Description: (Detail how the service addresses a specific problem)*

*Discover the Practical Benefit:*
*Practical Benefit (Identify and describe the practical benefits, such as increased efficiency, cost-saving, enhanced performance, etc.)*

*Differentiation:*
*(Explain how your service is different and better compared to other providers)*

*Describe the Emotional Benefit*
*Emotional Benefit:(Describe the emotional impact or benefit, such as feeling more secure, confident, happy, etc.)*

Selling services differs from selling products because your approach must be tailored to the unique problems or benefits each prospect seeks. Every call will require a customized strategy to address their specific needs.

In service sales, knowledge is truly power. The more you know, the better you can educate your prospects. When you educate them, you build trust—and trust leads to business.

At the end of this step, always pause to invite questions. Prospects will have queries, and you'll need to clarify or expand on certain points.

## Step 5: Build Trust

Now comes your favorite part: talking about how amazing you are.

After building value, it's time to build trust. Explain to the prospect why you're the go-to choice, and what sets you apart, and share examples of how you've delighted other customers.

Transition into this phase by "breaking the fourth wall."

In entertainment, the "fourth wall" refers to the imaginary barrier between the audience and the performers in a play or film. It's the boundary that separates the characters' fictional world from the audience's reality.

When performers acknowledge the audience or speak directly to them, they are "breaking the fourth wall." This technique can create humor, offer commentary, or strengthen the audience's connection with the characters.

Sales calls are similar. Everyone knows it's a sales call, but they often play along as if it's just a conversation. You can break the fourth wall by saying something like:

"Now that I've learned more about you and discussed some potential solutions, I'm going to switch into my sales mode and give you a quick elevator pitch. Well…maybe it's more like a ride up a few floors."

This reduces the tension around the inevitable offer that will be made, accepted, rejected, or questioned.

In this step, focus on building trust by sharing key points:

- How long the company has been around.
- How long you've been in this field.
- What you excel at compared to where others might compete with you.

- A summary of your key value propositions.
- Examples of satisfied clients, case studies, or any social proof.
- Awards, accreditations, licenses, or notable mentions.
- Your key differentiators.

The aim is to make them understand why the solutions you discussed in Step 4 are backed by solid evidence.

Highlight your strengths and what makes you unique.

Once you've covered these points, pause for questions.

Steps 4 and 5 involve a lot of you presenting. It's crucial to stop for questions to ensure clarity, address any concerns, and keep the prospect engaged.

This approach shows that you value their input throughout the discussion, encouraging them to listen more attentively.

This part of the sales call is about proving why you are who you say you are. Next, we move to what many call "the close," which varies depending on the product, service, or niche.

During the close, aim to alleviate any anxiety about the next steps, just as we did in step 2, by clearly outlining the path forward.

## Step 6: Light the Path Forward

During the close, your goal is to ease any anxiety about the next steps by clearly outlining what comes next, similar to what we did in step 2.

If you're selling a product, this is the moment to present your pricing. By now, you've built enough value and trust to confidently share the offer.

When you present the price, don't just say, "Our product/service costs $XXXX." Instead, use the Happy Formula to connect the price to the value you've built:

1. State the price.
2. Highlight the feature and what it does.
3. Explain how this feature benefits the prospect.
4. Describe how it solves their specific problem.
5. Illustrate the personal or business benefits they'll gain.

For example, instead of simply stating the price, you could say, "Our service is $XXXX. With that, you get [feature], which helps you [specific benefit]. This directly addresses your [problem] by [solution], ultimately providing you [personal/business benefit]."

There are a few possible reactions to presenting the price. They might agree and proceed, need time to consider or find the price too high. In any scenario, avoid pressuring them into an immediate decision. Some sales coaches advocate for a one-call close, but significant decisions often require more thought. Plus, your prospects have plenty of options and won't appreciate feeling pressured.

The Happy Selling System is designed for genuine interactions. Genuine people don't make others uncomfortable for their own gain.

After presenting the price, acknowledge the tension by saying:

"If you're ready to decide, just let me know. But for now, I'd like to explain our process."

This approach lets them think about their choice without feeling pressured to make a snap decision.

If you want to encourage them to act immediately, offer an incentive and explain why it benefits you both. For example, you might reduce the rate because acting now saves you money on follow-ups and communication. It's not about pressuring them; it's about presenting a practical reason for deciding sooner if they have all the information they need. Make it clear that there's no pressure, and the offer will remain available if they need more time.

Now, outline the next steps:

1. **What happens after the call?** Will you email them, call again, or follow up in another way? What's the timeline?
2. **Explain how to start doing business with you.** Do they pay an invoice, check out online, or need to call or visit you?
3. **Describe what it's like to do business with you.** How will they engage with your service or use your product in the first month?

This is an old sales technique called "assuming the sale," but done more gently here. You're helping them visualize what it's like to work with you. You might say:

"I'd like to help you visualize what it's like to work with us. Here's how we operate…"

If you're selling a product, explain what using it will be like.

By now, if you've followed each step, they should see you more as a guide than a salesperson. You're communicating, "This is the road ahead, and I'm here to walk you through it."

People deal with a lot of uncertainty in their lives, so it's comforting to have someone clearly outline the next steps.

Be that guide for your prospect.

When I sell my marketing services, I don't share pricing on the call because I'm in an ultra-competitive industry. Instead, I explain our process, what the next steps are, and how we engage. I also highlight what makes us different. Most of the call focuses on discovery.

One of my key next steps is to send a free preliminary marketing strategy along with our pricing.

This allows me to:

1. **Provide something of value** that competitors typically charge around $5,000 for. This sets me apart because I'm offering valuable insights at no cost.
2. **Alleviate anxiety about costs** by showing how I plan to scale their business, demonstrating my approach before they commit. This helps them see exactly how I think and ensures they're confident in my direction.
3. **Tap into the "Law of Reciprocity."** As described in Robert Cialdini's book "Influence: The Psychology of

Persuasion," this principle suggests people feel compelled to return favors. By offering something valuable upfront, I create a sense of obligation that encourages them to choose my services.

I make it clear to the client why I'm providing the free strategy: there's no catch. They're getting strong value because I believe we're the best choice and I'm willing to prove it. I might forgo $5,000 upfront, but this strategy can lead to earning $50,000+ from a long-term client relationship.

If you have something additional to provide that will add value after the call, like a special offer or a freebie, provide it.

High-pressure salespeople often underestimate their prospects, especially in B2B settings. Your prospects have likely read the same books, watched the same videos, and taken similar courses. Even in B2C, Gen Z customers can see insincerity. The best approach is to be genuine—not only because it's right but because it works better.

Before ending the call, ask a few key questions:

1. **What is your timeline for a decision?** Knowing this helps you plan follow-ups, manage your sales pipeline, and understand their commitment to a decision deadline. It also helps them mentally commit to a timeframe, preventing them from dragging out the decision.
2. **What is your budget?** This question is crucial when relevant. If you've already disclosed pricing, explain why

you need to know their budget. If you haven't, you can handle it in two ways:

- Explain that your rates are fixed and their budget won't affect the price. Let them know they can share their budget after seeing the proposal.
- Clarify why you need to know. For instance, in marketing services, the budget determines which channels to pursue and the level of testing possible. It's difficult to create a strategy and set goals without knowing the budget.

Finally, thank them for their time, mention something you enjoyed or admired from the conversation, summarize the next steps, and say goodbye.

If possible, get their consent to receive text messages from you, as these have the highest response rates. Just ensure you're not using your personal number for this.

## Step 7: Follow up

I once read a pest control brochure that said if you see one roach in your house, it likely means there are hundreds, if not thousands, hidden out of sight. The one you see is just the tip of the iceberg, pushed out because the others have taken over.

I apply this philosophy to personal and business relationships. If you notice a "cockroach" early in a relationship—when people are typically on their best behavior—it's a sign there could be many more problems lurking beneath the surface. This applies to dating, job interviews, and sales calls.

Spotting red flags early can save you a lot of trouble later.

Why am I bringing this up in the follow-up step? Because this is your first opportunity to prove to your prospect that you do what you say you're going to do.

They'll be watching to see if you stand by your word. If you promise to deliver something within 24 hours, ensure it arrives within 23 hours.

Always over-deliver, even if just by a small margin. If you don't, you'll only attract clients who also don't keep their promises, and those aren't the clients you want.

People tend to be more forgiving of faults they themselves possess. If you don't want to end up with procrastinators and clients who are unreliable, make sure you're not one of them.

The clients you want are punctual and dependable. They expect you to be as committed as they are.

This is the most crucial aspect of the follow-up.

You determine the timing and method of your follow-up, but here are some best practices:

1. **Send a Recap Email Immediately:**
   After the call, send a thank-you email recapping your discussion. This is a powerful gesture that shows appreciation and professionalism. It helps reinforce what was discussed, serves as a reminder for both of you, and shows you respect their time.

2. **Document Call Notes in Your CRM:**
   Always record your notes in a Customer Relationship Management (CRM) system. This is essential for staying organized and ensuring that nothing slips through the cracks.

3. **Include a Task List:**
   End your recap with a clear task list for both parties. For example, "(Prospect's name) to reach out with a decision by (date)." This keeps everything organized and clear, reducing the prospect's mental load. The easier you make it for them, the more likely they are to choose you.

4. **Fulfill Your Promises:**
   As discussed, this is your chance to demonstrate that you keep your word. Many salespeople miss deadlines or fail to follow up because they are burnt out. Don't be one of them. A significant portion of deals are lost at this stage.

5. **Follow Up Through Multiple Channels**
   If you don't hear back within the agreed timeline, follow up in this order: call, text, email.

   - **Call:** Tim Ferriss mentioned on his podcast that he prefers operating in less crowded spaces because it's easier to capture attention. Most salespeople don't follow up with a call anymore, making this a valuable opportunity. Even if they don't answer, leaving a voicemail adds a personal touch and has a greater impact than an email.

- **Text:** If calling doesn't work, send a text the next day. It's more direct and often gets quicker responses.
- **Email:** If they don't reply to your text, follow up with an email. End each email with a note on when they can expect your next follow-up if you don't hear back. This sets a mental trigger for them and keeps your follow-ups organized and predictable.

Most salespeople rely heavily on email, which can be easily ignored. By following up with calls and texts first, you're more likely to get a response.

If email is your only option, make sure each one is well-crafted and always communicate when you will follow up next. This approach helps keep you on their radar without being intrusive.

In essence, be the guide your prospects can trust by showing them you follow through on your promises. Consistently demonstrate reliability and professionalism, and you'll win their business by becoming a source of relief in their busy lives.

# Happy Prospecting Process

Sometimes you're fortunate enough to receive high-quality inbound leads, either through your own efforts or from a diligent marketing team. I'm lucky that my leads are typically high-intent; by the time they reach me, they've scheduled a 30-60-minute video call and provided all the information I need to understand their company before our meeting. This makes it much easier to follow the process and implement The Happy Sales System effectively.

However, it wasn't always this smooth when I started my first business. Back then, I had to actively seek out and generate leads. Before I could get to the actual sales call, I needed to engage in what's often called prospecting. This involves reaching out to cold or lukewarm leads to transform them into warm or hot leads who are willing to take a sales call.

Prospecting follows a similar process to the main sales call but has its nuances that can significantly impact your success in converting leads into sales.

## Know What You're Selling

When prospecting, it's crucial to understand what you're selling. This might seem obvious, but many people mistakenly try to sell the product, service, or company during the initial prospecting call. That's not the objective here. Your primary goal is to sell getting on the the sales call itself. You're selling the appointment, not your offer. You need to clearly articulate why this call will benefit them and entice them to agree to it.

## Have an Offer

To capture people's attention and get them to commit to a call, you need to provide a compelling reason. My team offers a free content marketing strategy to prospects willing to jump on a sales call with us. While this seemed like a substantial offer upfront, it cost us nothing because it was a service we provided after every sales call anyway. This creates a win/win situation.

Identify your unique value proposition and use it as an incentive.

Develop an offer that's hard to refuse, one that can provide long-term ROI and positions you as the solution to their problem(s).

## Craft the Pitch

Once you're clear that your objective is to secure the appointment and you have a compelling offer, it's time to craft your pitch.

A well-structured pitch typically includes the following components:

## Intro

Start with a proper introduction. Make sure you clearly state who you are and why you're calling. If the prospect is left wondering "Who?" After your introduction, you've missed the mark. I've seen this happen in many sales consultations, and it might be a familiar scenario to you.

"Hi this is (salesperson) calling with (company name)
Customer: Who?
Salesperson: (company name)
Customer: Who?
Salesperson: (company name)
Customer: ok"

This is NOT the way to start a sales call. Immediately alleviate any uncertainty about what this call is about and where it's going.

The way to introduce yourself is "Hi, this is (salesperson name), I don't need more than (x minutes of your time), I'm calling with (company name) and we (provide this main product/service/solution/benefit to our customers) - the reason I'm calling is (offer)."

You never want to just make a statement, so after everything you say, ask a question to continue the conversation. Even if it's something as simple as: Does that sound like something you would be interested in hearing more about?

You can also ask if they are dealing with (problems you solve) at the moment.

This reminds them they have a problem.

Also, it may be obvious to some, but just in case it's not, this intro happens after you've politely asked them how they are doing today.

## If They Say No - 2nd Attempt

If the initial pitch is declined, make one more effort by framing a different problem/solution statement and give it another try. For example, you might say:

"I understand that some people in your niche face (x problem). At our company, we address this by (solution), and our approach has helped other companies achieve (x results). This call will only take (x time), and even if it doesn't meet your needs, you'll still gain (something of value that costs them nothing)."

If they still decline, offer to add them to your email marketing list. This way, you can nurture their interest over time. If they agree, include them in a list for your marketing team to add to a nurture campaign—indicating there's interest but the timing might not be right.

Remember, you only want to make one extra effort. A well-communicated offer gives enough information for a potential client to decide if they want to learn more. The Happy Selling System is about maintaining a positive experience for both parties and respecting their boundaries. Our goal is not to be intrusive or disrupt their day.

## If They Say Yes - Discovery

If they accept, grab at least a few hot buttons or pain points that will aid you in the sales call.

Communicate your intention for asking the next question. Ask your prospect a few questions about their problem and how it impacted them.

It can go something like this:

"If it's okay with you, I'd like to ask a few questions that will help me make sure our booked call is a productive one, can you tell me a little more about (the problem you solved) and how you are dealing with it at the moment"

This reminds them they have this problem, and gives you something to prepare for the call.

Be genuine and have a conversation here. You'd be surprised how being relaxed and natural can affect your voice and a prospect's receptiveness to you. Genuinely take an interest in them and you'll know if you need to ask 1 question or 10 questions. Your goal is not to sell, it's to help.

## Book the Time

Once you learn a bit more about them, tie in a snippet as to how you see that problem being solved and immediately transition into a calendar appointment.

"Perfect, I'd like to get something on the books for us. How does (providing two time slots on two different days) sound?"

Once they give you a time, actively fill out the calendar invite, confirm their email and contact information, and make sure they get the calendar invite to the call.

## Light the Path Forward

Always end any sales engagement with this. Alleviate the anxiety of the next step and establish yourself as a guide by lighting the path forward. The prospect must always be confident they are aware of what happens next, and should never be filled with uncertainty. It's your job to make them confident.

"I sent over that calendar invite, here is what you can expect next:

1. We will have our call on (date and time ) for (intention)
2. You will derive this benefit
3. This is what will happen after

Do you have any questions for me?"

End the call.

## Sell the Sales Call

I can't stress enough to not go into a full pitch of your product or service. Only the solution, the benefit, and the offer.

Your job is to get the appointment and avoid going into the sale unless they want you to.

The only way you jump into the sales call is if the prospect tells you they have time now.

Here is the condensed script version for reference:

**Sales Script**

***Introduction:***

*Salesperson:*
*Hi I was looking for [Prospect Name]?*

*Hi [Prospect Name],*
*How are you?*

*Salesperson:*
*Hi, this is [Salesperson Name] from [Company Name]. We provide [main product/service/solution/benefit to our customers]. The reason I'm calling is [offer].*

*Customer:*
*[Responds]*

*Salesperson:*
*Great to hear!*

*Are you currently [addressing a problem] at your company, if so, how? (or) Does that sound like something you would be interested in hearing more about?*

*If They Say No - 2nd Attempt:*

*Salesperson:*
*I understand. Just to give you a bit more context, I know some people in your niche face [X problem], and we solve this by [solution]. Other companies have seen [X results] implemented. The call would only take [X time], and if it's not of value to you, at least you walk away with [something of value that costs them nothing]. Does that sound better?*

*Customer:*
*[Responds]*

*Salesperson:*
*(If they say no again)*

*Would you like me to add you to our email list to keep you updated with valuable insights and offers?*
*If they say yes to the email, add them to the list for your marketing team to nurture.*

*(If They Say Yes) - Discovery*

*Salesperson:*
*Great! If it's okay with you, I'd like to ask a few questions that will help me make sure our booked call is productive. Can you tell me a little more about [the problem you solve] and how you are handling it now?*

*Customer:*
*[Responds]*

*Salesperson:*
*Be genuine and have a conversation here. Your goal is not to sell, but to help.*

*Book the Time:*

*Salesperson:*
*Perfect, I'd like to get something on the books for us. How does [provide two time slots on two different days] sound?*

*Customer:*
*[Responds with a time]*

*Salesperson:*
*Great, I'll send you a calendar invite right now. Can I confirm your email and contact info?*

*Make sure they get the calendar invite on the call.*
*Light the Path Forward:*

*Salesperson:*
*I sent over that calendar invite. Here's what you can expect next:*

1. *We will have our call on [date and time] for [intention].*
2. *You will derive this benefit [specific benefit].*
3. *This will happen after [next steps].*

*Do you have any questions for me?*

*Customer:*
*[Responds]*

*Salesperson:*
*Thank you, looking forward to our meeting!*

The goal is to keep both parties happy and within moral boundaries. Happy selling!

# Happy Sales Principles

Using The Happy Sales System can transform you into a happy, stress-free, and high-performing salesperson. By integrating this approach into your sales process, you'll not only convert more deals but also feel good throughout the sales journey.

This system is designed for today's educated consumer, who is often put off by the outdated "used car" sales tactics of the 90s or the aggressive call center approaches from the early 2000s.

However, to make this system truly effective, there are essential tips, tricks, and principles you need to incorporate throughout the process. Some of these are naturally covered if you follow the system, while others require a more deliberate focus.

Let's explore a few key principles that you must follow to become a happy and successful salesperson. While some of these have been woven into the process already, it's worth delving into them in more detail.

## Acknowledge the Fourth Wall

As mentioned, the fourth wall is the unspoken reality that everyone knows: this is a business transaction. Yet, no one usually acknowledges it openly. Disarm your prospects by being upfront about this truth.

Whenever you have to pitch, offer an incentive, or engage in any obvious selling, call it out.

This approach isn't just fluff—it's genuinely effective. Here are some practical examples of how to use this strategy:

### Offering an Incentive for Immediate Action

When you offer an incentive for acting now, explain the real reason behind it. For example, say, "I'm providing this incentive because it saves me time and money on follow-ups, and I want to pass those savings on to you."

This approach differs from simply saying, "Act now to get a discount." If you don't explain, customers might feel pressured and suspect that you're just being pushy and that they won't get the same price later.

The reality is far less sinister: incentive exists because it benefits both parties. It saves time and money for everyone involved and allows the customer to start enjoying the product or service sooner.

### Discounts for Multi-Month Payments

When offering discounts for paying upfront for multiple months, explain why. You might say, "We provide discounts for multi-month payments because it helps create a predictable revenue stream for the year, allowing us to allocate resources more effectively to deliver our services."

## Giving Something for Free

When you offer something for free, prospects often think there's a hidden agenda or a catch. Disarm this suspicion by saying, "I'm giving you this freebie because I want you to see how we stand out from your competitors. We care more about earning your business because we know our product/service is superior."

## Discussing Pricing Upfront

A common question is about the price upfront. Instead of the typical, vague response, be honest: "I don't like to give a price upfront because I haven't had a chance to explain the value yet. I want you to understand what you're getting before we discuss the cost. If I just give you a price, you won't know if it's worth it. But by the end of our conversation today, you will know the price."

Robert Cialdini, in his book "Influence: The Psychology of Persuasion," highlights a study by social psychologist Ellen Langer that underscores the power of giving a reason, even if it's a weak one. In her experiment, people were asked to cut in line to use a photocopy machine with three different approaches:

**No Reason:** "Excuse me, I have 5 pages. May I use the Xerox machine?"

**Good Reason:** "Excuse me, I have 5 pages. May I use the Xerox machine because I'm in a rush?"

**Placebo Reason**: "Excuse me, I have 5 pages. May I use the Xerox machine because I have to make some copies?"

The results showed that without a reason, 60% allowed the person to cut in line. With a good reason, compliance increased to 94%. Surprisingly, with a placebo reason, compliance was still high at 93%. This experiment demonstrated that simply providing a reason, even if it's weak, can significantly increase compliance.

While I'm not suggesting you give a weak reason, always provide a reason for your actions. Decades of sketchy sales tactics have linked sales with dishonesty. Show that you're different—not just because it's effective, but because it's the right thing to do.

Communicate your intentions clearly and truthfully. Whatever is genuine to you, make sure to express it honestly.

## Pre-Buttal, Not Rebuttal

Sales trainers often focus heavily on objections and rebuttals, spending days or even weeks equipping their teams with verbal judo moves to counter every possible objection.

The problem with this approach is that it trains salespeople to see objections as attacks rather than opportunities to educate their customers. An objection usually manifests as a question, and questions are a clear sign of interest. If you're hearing "objections," it means your prospect is engaged and paying attention.

Instead of viewing objections as attacks, consider them valuable learning opportunities for both you and your prospect. For your prospect, because you have the opportunity to provide additional information. For you, because it signals that you may not have provided enough information initially. Whenever you encounter an objection, take it as a cue to incorporate the response into all future sales calls.

This is where the concept of pre-buttal comes in. Your sales presentation should strategically address potential objections before they even arise.

## Examples of Pre-buttal:

Higher Pricing Compared to Competitors

If you know your pricing is higher than your competitors, address it upfront when discussing pricing:

"Our pricing is a bit higher than what you might see elsewhere because we offer [this additional benefit] by working with us."

Even if this wasn't going to be an objection, it's something they'll likely discover during their research phase. Remember, everyone has access to search engines. Transparency isn't just ethical—it's unavoidable in today's information-rich world.

When you address an objection before it's raised, you achieve several key outcomes:

## Build Professionalism and Trust

By proactively discussing potential concerns, you show that you understand your product and industry deeply and can handle tough topics without being asked. This establishes a level of professionalism and trust that other vendors might not provide.

### Soothe Quiet Prospects' Concerns

Not all prospects voice their objections or questions. Some may have concerns but won't express them, especially if they're less assertive. Addressing these issues upfront ensures that even quiet prospects feel their concerns are resolved, rather than leaving them unspoken and unresolved.

### Remove the "Attack/Defend" Dynamic

By preemptively addressing objections, you shift away from the adversarial nature of typical sales calls, creating a more collaborative and comfortable dialogue.

To effectively integrate this approach, write down all the objections and questions you've encountered and weave them into your Happy Sales presentation.

## Pressure to Speak is On You

One of the most important things to know as a salesperson is that the pressure to keep the conversation going is always on you. Being a good salesperson means being an effective communicator.

Good communicators can keep conversations flowing naturally. In any communication, take on the role of the guide. You're in charge.

Your job is to make people feel comfortable and at ease. This means they should have to do as little thinking as possible.

Never conclude with just a statement. Always keep the conversation progressing or ask a question. For example, after breaking the ice (Step 1), smoothly transition by explaining the structure of the call:

"Let me tell you how this call will go…"

Once you've outlined the call, move on to a question (Step 3):

"Can you tell me a bit more about yourself and what prompted this call?"

After gathering their responses and building value, continue by asking:

"Based on what I've shared, do you have any questions before I tell you more about us?"

This approach not only keeps the conversation going but also gives them space to express themselves and reassures them about the next steps, easing any anxiety about what's coming.

Always maintain a calm and confident demeanor, letting the prospect know you're in control and that they can trust you to lead the way. Building this sense of trust during the conversation will create a positive perception of what it will be like to work with you.

If you find yourself at a loss for words after making a statement, simply ask, "How does that sound?" Then proceed to the next step.

If they pose a question unexpectedly, follow up with, "Did I answer your question well?" and then smoothly return to your process.

The responsibility to keep the conversation engaging and flowing rests on you.

## Always Be Enthusiastic

In Frank Bettger's book, How I Raised Myself from Failure to Success in Selling, one of his key tips for achieving success in sales is to show enthusiasm. He emphasizes that enthusiasm is crucial because it is contagious and can influence your prospects to become more interested in your offer. This principle remains timeless advice for anyone in sales.

During my time working at a high-volume sales call center, I pitched to dozens of people every day. This constant interaction provided me with a significant data set each day, week, and month, allowing me to see what was effective and what wasn't.

Interestingly, my pitch didn't change much day to day. The words I used were consistent. What varied was how I felt. I noticed that on days when I was "on" and energetic, I closed more deals. Conversely, on days when I was feeling down, I often didn't close any deals at all. It wasn't just that my closing rate was lower—it was non-existent.

In these calls, clients could only judge me by my voice, not my body language or facial expressions. My tone made a significant impact on my sales outcomes.

I realized that on days when my energy was low, I would slump in my chair, smile less during calls, speak more slowly, and generally sound less enthusiastic. These actions turned a "bad day" into a self-fulfilling prophecy.

To succeed in sales, you need to radiate positive energy and be genuinely enthusiastic about what you're selling. If you can't get excited about your offer, you can't expect your customers to either. Let your passion shine through.

However, this enthusiasm must be genuine. You can't fake it. Customers can sense when you're being disingenuous, just like they can spot the so-called "customer service voice" from a mile away. There's a reason it's not called a "sales voice." People are naturally intuitive. Even if they can't pinpoint why, they will sense when something feels off and might mistrust you.

I once received a cold call about lead generation software. The caller was so calm and laid-back that I didn't have my usual gut reaction of, "Oh no, another sales call ruining my day." Normally, this reaction is a mix of irritation and the urge to reject the call immediately, regardless of the offer.

However, the caller's relaxed and genuine demeanor caught my attention. I gave him a chance, and it turned out his product was just what my business needed. This single call resulted in $10,000 in annual revenue for them—all because the caller was confident and sincere. He knew the value of what he was offering and didn't project any fear.

The essence of The Happy Sales System is that everyone involved should be happy. To achieve this, you need to be a good, genuine human being. This means not taking out your frustrations on others. Whether you had a rough night because of your kids or personal issues, we all face challenges. But it doesn't justify giving half-hearted effort or ruining someone else's day.

One of the best pieces of advice I've heard recently comes from MMA fighter Kamaru Usman. In an interview, he shared a wisdom his mother used to impart during tough times:

"If we all put our problems in a pile, you would take yours back and run."

Facing challenges is an opportunity to develop empathy for others who might be experiencing similar or even worse difficulties. Never assume you're the only one struggling, and always strive to put your best foot forward in your interactions with others.

## Follow up

One of the biggest factors affecting the close rate isn't just the sales call itself but the follow-up process. By the end of the initial call, most prospects have a sense of whether they want to work with you. However, deals are often lost due to inadequate follow-up or the absence of it altogether.

To ensure a successful follow-up, there are a few key steps to follow:

### Always Set a Follow-Up Date

During the initial conversation, ask your prospect when they would prefer you to follow up. This sets a clear expectation and commits both you and the client to a specific date. If they can't provide a date, suggest one yourself.

## Reverse the Typical Communication Order

Start with a call, then send a text, and finally, an email. Many people begin with an email and only escalate if they don't get a response. Flip this approach.

Since few salespeople use the phone anymore, calling first gives you an edge by using a less crowded communication channel. When you call, be polite, break the ice with some small talk, and ease into the conversation before discussing business. This approach isn't just effective—it's good manners.

Implement a Structured Follow-Up Cadence: If your prospect is unresponsive after the initial call, follow a consistent follow-up schedule. A good approach might be:

5 calls in the morning
5 calls in the evening
5-7 emails
3 text messages

Spread these over 3-4 weeks

If you still don't hear from them after this period, mark them as "lost" and place them into a monthly nurture campaign.

As someone who often becomes a lead for services I need, I notice when salespeople follow up. Sometimes, I'm simply too busy to respond immediately. A good salesperson will understand this and will call again or reach out through another medium, allowing me to respond at a more convenient time.

As a business owner, my days are packed. When I'm shopping around for different services or products, the salesperson with the most diligent and effective follow-up usually wins my business.

## Don't Disappear After the Sale

Stay in touch with your customers even after the sale. If you've done a good job during the sales process, your customers will likely feel a stronger connection with you than with the service team. By reaching out, you make them feel valued as individuals rather than just transactions.

This ongoing contact can also provide valuable insights into their experiences. Whether the feedback is positive or negative, it's crucial to hear it. Positive feedback can bolster your confidence and strategies, while constructive criticism can be used to improve your pitch or provide useful input to the product team.

Additionally, staying connected with your customers deepens your relationship with them. This can lead to referrals, and at the very least, create more loyal customers who are less likely to churn.

## Play the Numbers

If you're a startup or a solopreneur, one critical lesson you may not have learned yet is that sales is fundamentally a numbers game.

Yes, there are strategies to improve your close rate. Following these processes can help you achieve a close rate above 50%. However, these strategies are meant to enhance your close rate, not establish one from scratch.

I've consulted with many startup companies that have reported no sales. Initially, you might suspect there's an issue with their offer or product. However, after a few questions, it often becomes clear that their outreach is limited—barely reaching 100 calls, with actual conversations in the single or double digits. We're not even talking about sales calls, just basic conversations.

Even if you're inexperienced or unskilled in sales, there's usually a "laydown" in your lead pool. A laydown is a prospect so eager and in need of your product or service that they're ready to buy regardless of your pitch. If you haven't encountered your laydown yet, you simply haven't reached out to enough people.

Improving your close rate and the number of conversations you have is beneficial, but you need to start by generating volume, even if the initial close rate is low.

You need to increase your outreach—get your product or service in front of a significant number of people, and you will start to see buyers emerge. As you gain more customers, you'll become better at identifying the types of people who are most likely to buy from you, allowing you to target them more effectively.

Let your sales efforts inform your marketing strategies and vice versa.

Many sales experts rightly emphasize the importance of volume. A good starting point is a minimum of 100 calls and 100 emails per day for each salesperson. Maintain this level of activity for a few months to build your pipeline before assessing your campaign's success. Remember, each industry has its own sales cycle—some close deals within a week, while others may take several months. Avoid making premature assumptions; focus on doing the work and being patient.

This approach is akin to what Joshua Medcalf discusses in his book, Chop Wood, Carry Water: How to Fall in Love with the Process of Becoming Great. Medcalf highlights the importance of committing to daily tasks rather than obsessing over the end goal. Apply this philosophy to your sales outreach. Just as consistently chopping wood and carrying water leads to growth, daily sales activities like making calls, sending emails, and following up with leads are crucial. Dedicate time each day to these tasks for you or your team, and you will see progress. Like any skill, you'll improve with practice.

Immerse yourself in the process, and you will see your numbers rise.

If you've managed to sell to even a handful of people, your lack of revenue isn't due to a lack of value in your offering—it's because you haven't shown it to enough people. Once you reach a large enough audience, you can establish a baseline for how many interactions lead to a sale. With this baseline, you can refine your communication to increase your success rate, using principles like those in The Happy Sales System.

## Track the Numbers

Whether you're a founder, sales manager, or salesperson, it's common to struggle with tracking sales effectively.

Typically, sales teams take all leads from various channels, lump them into one pipeline, and establish a baseline close rate. However, reality is more nuanced.

Each marketing channel delivers leads with different levels of intent. Let's break it down with an example:

Salesperson 1 handles organic search leads.
Salesperson 2 manages paid social media leads.
Salesperson 3 focuses on cold outreach leads.

It's unrealistic to expect all these salespeople to have the same close rate.

The truth is, prospects from each channel vary in their intent, knowledge, and position within the marketing funnel. This means each group requires a different approach to move them towards making a purchase.

Even if all leads are distributed randomly among the sales team or funneled to one person, it's crucial to track the close rate of each channel separately.

By doing this, you can identify which channel provides the highest quality leads.

This way, if your marketing changes and the close rate drops, you won't mistakenly blame your sales team for a lack of enthusiasm.

Additionally, avoid tracking efforts too early. When you introduce a new channel, you're essentially creating a new pipeline with its own unique cycle. Don't rush to judge a marketing or sales campaign until you've established an average time to close. Let this average run three times before making a final assessment.

## Make the Most of the Numbers

In Malcolm Gladwell's book "Outliers," he introduces the "10,000 Hour Rule," suggesting that becoming an expert in any field generally requires about 10,000 hours of practice. However, this idea has often been misunderstood to mean that merely spending a lot of time practicing is sufficient for mastery. Geoff Colvin, in his book "Talent is Overrated," argues that what truly matters is "deliberate practice."

Colvin describes deliberate practice as a focused and structured activity aimed at improving performance. It involves constant feedback, working on weaknesses, and repeating challenging tasks that are just beyond one's current abilities. This type of practice is mentally demanding and not always enjoyable, but it leads to significant improvement and mastery.

Gladwell's view on the 10,000-hour rule overlooks this crucial aspect. It's not just about the quantity of hours spent; it's about how those hours are utilized. Colvin emphasizes that without deliberate practice, simply putting in the time won't lead to excellence. The key point is that structured, purposeful practice with clear goals and feedback is what truly drives high performance, not just the volume of practice hours.

Deliberate, focused practice is essential to achieving excellence in sales.

Why am I sharing this after saying that "sales is a numbers game"?

While sales do involve numbers, relying solely on volume to compensate for weaknesses isn't effective. The purpose of making numerous sales calls is twofold:

1. Increase your sales.
2. Improve your ability to make sales.

You won't get better at sales without deliberate practice. As mentioned above, improvement comes not just from doing, but from intentionally trying to enhance your skills.

The best way to improve is to review your calls. You'd be surprised at how much you can learn about your sales techniques when you do this.

When you listen to your calls, you'll notice when prospects share valuable insights with you. You'll become aware of your speaking patterns and whether you interrupt prospects just as they're about to provide key information needed to close the sale. You might realize you talk too much or too little. You may also notice excessive use of filler words like "uhm" or discover that your headset has poor audio quality, making your voice either piercing or barely audible. An easy way to record calls without alarming your prospect is to use a notetaker AI.

Improvement is impossible without evaluating your calls, whether by yourself or someone else. All sales interactions—be it calls, emails, chats, or texts—should be assessed.

I once visited a software company's website and started chatting with their sales team. I explained that I was comparing their product to competitors and asked how they differed.

The salesperson told me to "check their features page for that information."

They lost $6,000 a year to their competitor that day, just from me. Imagine how often that happens daily. They're likely leaving 6 to 7 figures of additional revenue on the table with salespeople like that. If no one monitors it, no one can improve it.

This could be happening to you.

Focus on volume, but also dedicate time each day or week to evaluate how you're executing within that volume.

You can double or triple your closed deals by taking the time to deliberately practice the craft of communication. You have the power to double your income without doubling your volume, simply by refining your process.

# Maintain Mental and Physical Health

Consistency in your process, consistency in prospecting, consistency in following up, consistency in enthusiasm, and consistency in deliberate practice. To maintain this level of consistency, you must also be consistent in your physical and mental health, for which you bear the responsibility.

No, I'm not suggesting you need a six-pack or to jump on testosterone therapy like some advocate. That's not true health. Health is about keeping your body and mind in a condition where you can perform well every day. It's not how you look.

Many salespeople are stressed and burnt out, which is why there's such high turnover in this career. High-pressure sales tactics can feel unnatural and add to the stress, which then gets taken home, leading to unhealthy coping mechanisms. It's disheartening to see salespeople guzzling 3-4 energy drinks or 6-10 cups of coffee a day. It doesn't take that to succeed in sales. When you rely on these crutches, you're not finding the energy to talk to people; you're just coping with a process that feels unnatural to you.

I'm not a health guru, and I'm not going to propose a 12-week weight loss plan, but there are simple, effective things you should be doing.

### Get Your Sleep

Sleep should be your top priority. Instead of setting an alarm to wake up, set an alarm to go to bed. One of the best ways to ensure good, restful sleep is to avoid stimulants in the afternoon.

When you get good sleep, you'll be less stressed, more energetic, and healthier—all of which will be evident to your prospects. I find that the days I sleep well are the days I perform at my best, both for myself and those around me.

There is no substitute for sleep. Make sure you have enough.

**Get Your Rest**

Rest isn't the same as sleep. We're not robots, and we can't work from sunup to sundown, no matter what some motivational speakers claim. I've met a few of them, and their idea of "16-hour days" often just means being awake for 16 hours, which we all do.

Success in any field isn't about working all the time or for how long; it's about how effective you are during the time you do work.

Managing your energy is more important than managing your time. You can accomplish more in one focused hour than in two hours of low-energy effort.

Take short breaks during your workday away from screens. After work, do something you love.

Hard work has diminishing returns. It can even hurt results because we become less effective as we get more tired.

The intensity of your work is more important than how long you work.

**Limit the Stimulants**

Salespeople often abuse stimulants like coffee, nicotine, and smart drugs. Limit intake and keep it consistent. I'm not telling you to quit everything and become a zen master, but if you use stimulants, take the same dose at the same time every day. This helps your body and brain find a consistent baseline. Knowing your daily output allows you to plan your work around it without burning out.

Salespeople quit due to burnout, not because "sales is hard." Yes, sales has its challenges, but it's an incredibly rewarding profession. Most of the stress you experience is the mental and physical stress you place on yourself.

**Exercise**

Humans are designed to move. Physical activity helps release the physical stress that builds up in our bodies.

No matter your fitness level or how busy you are, everyone can do this:

Set a timer for 5 minutes. Do as many push-ups or squats as you can within those 5 minutes. Do each set to failure, rest no more than 30 seconds, and repeat until the timer runs out.

This routine requires no gym, takes less time than you spend scrolling through social media, and you can do it even if you're feeling low on energy.

## Don't Take it Personally

Never take sales personally. You'll meet many people with diverse personalities and quirks. Not everyone will be nice, you'll hear more "no's" than "yes's," and sometimes people might even take out their bad day on you.

Not every "yes" is worth pursuing, and every "no" serves a purpose. Remember, your work is not who you are; it's just what you do.

View sales for what it is—a game. The best way to excel at it is to enjoy playing it.

# The Ceiling is You

One of the most amazing things about the sales profession is that you are only limited by what you can do. You get to control how much growth you have and how much money you make, which isn't something a lot of professions can say.

Salespeople get to "eat what they kill" and not what's given to them.

The upside is that you get to control your ceiling. You can control how far you can go.

That is also the downside. You don't just get paid for being physically present; you get paid for performing.

When done right, it can be an incredibly rewarding profession. It can be even more rewarding if you feel good about how you earn your living.

That's what this system will help you do.

# A Message to Salespeople

If you could only take away one thing from this book, it would be this: be a genuine human being and treat prospects accordingly. If you truly view the prospect as a friend, you will not only guide them but also help them figure out if they need this product or service.

Good salesmanship is more empathy than manipulation. Everything you do in The Happy Selling System centers around the end consumer. Even the "tricks" you use are designed to help them make a decision, not force them to commit to one. It's a process where everyone achieves their desired outcomes from the engagement.

Many treat each sale as if it were their last. This pressure leads them to do and say unethical things to close the deal. It also makes them focus solely on the front-end numbers of "deals closed," but that's not all that matters in sales.

You have to consider the intangibles that aren't immediately visible. How did you make the prospect feel? Did they like you? Would they refer you to someone they know?

If you weren't in the room, what would they say about you? Did they truly need what you have to offer?

Scarcity drives people to act at their worst. Almost always, scarcity is an illusion. If you need an example, think back to the videos of people fighting over toilet paper during the pandemic. Physically fighting each other. For toilet paper.

Remember, there is enough for everyone to catch a fish. There is enough for everyone to eat. It's not you versus anyone else.

It's us. In this together. Always.

Live in the truth, and the truth is that this world is abundant.

As the great Zig Ziglar said: "You can have everything in life you want if you will just help enough other people get what they want."

That is your job as a salesperson.

# A Message to Business Owners

Sales doesn't have to be a revolving door. People naturally want to be kind and genuine, and there is a way to sell that aligns with their true selves. Allow your salespeople to leverage what makes them unique—their personality. Not everyone has to be your carbon copy. Don't give them a script that fits your personality and expect them all to feel comfortable using it.

More importantly, integrate this approach not only into your sales process but also into how you treat your salespeople. Training and feedback sessions don't have to be high-pressure environments of criticism. Instead, treat your salespeople as you would if your customers were right there in the room, observing your interactions.

Love your employees as you love your customers. You can't have one without the other. They are human beings too, and they deserve to be happy.

Help them achieve their goals, and they will help you achieve yours.

## What I Know About You

You're a winner because you're doing something that most salespeople, and people in general, don't do: you strive to be better. This desire alone will take you far, helping you to become your best and stand out from the crowd.

Keep nurturing this thirst for knowledge. Read every sales book you can find, good or bad. Each one is a resource and a pathway to ideas that can transform your life.

You're not willing to win "by any means necessary." Instead, you're committed to doing it the right way, without losing sleep at night from guilt or self-loathing.

What many people don't realize is that this approach leads to a more abundant and peaceful life. You won't have to worry about anything negative coming back around, because what will return to you is the positivity you've shared.

You are the small change the world needs. You are the ripple that can help steer humanity in the right direction, away from cold capitalism and towards conscious capitalism, where we understand that we are all here together and should take care of each other.

# Happy Selling

I hope that this book helps you find more happiness in your professional life. That you realize you can be yourself, you can be kind, be genuine, be you, and win at life. Never let the world scare you into thinking otherwise.

# About the Author

**Sean Dudayev** is a distinguished expert in sales and marketing, with over 18 years of experience in the field. As the founder of Frootful Marketing, Sean has dedicated his career to empowering entrepreneurs and businesses to achieve exceptional sales success. His extensive background in sales has equipped him with a deep understanding of complexities and nuances of the sales process.

Sean has consulted with hundreds of entrepreneurs, providing them with actionable insights and strategies to enhance their sales and marketing efforts. His expertise lies in his ability to combine deep industry knowledge with a modern understanding of consumer behavior. This fusion has led to the development of a straightforward yet powerful 7-step process designed to make salespeople not only more successful but also genuinely happier in their roles.

Throughout his career, Sean has been a strong advocate for authentic, customer-focused sales approaches. He believes that true sales mastery comes from building meaningful relationships and truly understanding the needs of clients, rather than relying on high-pressure tactics. This philosophy is central to his teachings and the systems he creates.

Sean's work with Frootful Marketing embodies his commitment to helping businesses thrive in today's competitive market. His innovative and empathetic approach to sales and marketing continues to inspire professionals to achieve their highest potential, fostering a culture of success and satisfaction in their sales endeavors.

He can be reached for inquiries at
[Sean@FrootfulMarketing.com](mailto:Sean@FrootfulMarketing.com)

www.ingramcontent.com/pod-product-compliance
Lightning Source LLC
Chambersburg PA
CBHW070124230526
45472CB00004B/1408